AF423086

ETCHED IN A TIME OF RECKONING

MARK MCGRAIN

ETCHED IN A TIME OF RECKONING

IMMERSION RECORDS & MEDIA

NEW ORLEANS, LOUISIANA USA

Immersion Records & Media is an independent publishing house located in
New Orleans, U.S.A.

Print ISBN: 979-8-218-29135-8
eBook ISBN: 979-8-218-29137-2

Library of Congress Control Number:
2023949279
Names: McGrain, Mark, author.
Title: Etched In A Time Of Reckoning / Mark McGrain
Identifiers: LCCN 2023949279 | ISBN 9798218291358 (pbk.)
LC record available at https://lccn.loc.gov/2023949279

1st Edition

IMMERSION RECORDS & MEDIA
1013 Saint Anthony Street
New Orleans, Lousiana 70116
www.immersionrecords.com

www.markmcgrain.com

In memory of
Teresa McGrain
(1898 - 1994)

CONTENTS

Omnia mutantur, nihil interit.

  --Ovid (43 BC - 17 AD)

(Everything changes, nothing perishes.)

Vacillant Tide

Bumbershoots sprout
from a bamboo's potted stand,
guarding the entrance
to a water shed ambush.

Break-wall harboring
thoughts lost to the sea,
near forgotten loves
in far forbidden ports.

Rain gushes off rooftops,
splashing hard upon Chartres Street,
a refill, poured freely
of a suitor's crimson cup:

"The money," you whisper,
"is nothing but for wine and reefer,
and pornography spilled out
upon the living room floor."

Spilled out upon this table
of cool, clear marble,
porcelain bud vase erect,
as thoughts heave heavily,
drowned deep beneath
a dank and darkened breast.

I burst wildly into the street,
dodging down-spouts,
luring flooded storm drains
like a raging torrent upon Jackson Square,
Mimes and Tarot readers sent
helplessly washing downstream
in the swift and furious current.

But the bells of Saint Louis Cathedral

clang a merciful beacon:
fending shipwrecks,
channeling safe passage
to those whose fortunes
float patiently bobbing
on the quieted surface
of a hushed, still vacillant tide.

Rain Gracefully Bows

The rain gracefully bows
for coffin flies to come pouring
through the open window:

Now's not good; go back (but can't)
wrapped tightly in ashen grey cocoon, silent
dark, dank, musty of rotting flotsam
strewn along the beach's highest mark,
the highest of any tide
ever known, receded.

The stink from rotting meat and seafood,
Frigidaires lost and leaning open,
nails upright in the streets,
sparks arcing at dusk,
an occasional boat fallen to earth.
dogs prowling on three legs emaciated,
towing gnawed-off ropes and broken chains:
dangling snares locked to their throats,
can't swallow, starving
and soon to die.

They come in swarms
to graze the dead and disabled,
these flies freshly hatched of ancient dung,
racing up one's nose
or rushing in past a yawn;
infesting the dreams of the sleeping
even while the seventh ward continues to decay,
empty to air its stubborn last, alone
'til rain returns to wash the mold
from sand, rubble, glass,
and crimson stained broken clay.

Ghostly Meanderings

Salt fallen drifts
atop ancient ruins
older than Europe
stained anew still
glistening in the same sunrise
enlightened by the familiar procession
of both measureless jubilation
and well-marked remorse;
the place where this country came to die.

Aloft in New Orleans attics,
resounding voices, spirit trombones
lyrically conjuring the childless heirs,
last survivors of the Jazz Age
performing songs of the forebearers,
stubbornly staving silence,
refusing to pass before the hand-off
not understanding that this time
no one's left standing
to carry on.

Ancestral bellowing
over rooftops, down alleys,
echoing like flat stones skipping,
skimming the glistening surface,
each hop shorter than the last,
in steady diminuendo then gone,
ghostly meanderings crisscrossing the top water
of the lower Mississippi
as it flushes soul after promising soul
slipping downstream
toward the gulf.

Saint Anthony and Burgundy

Italy and France collide
in Faubourg Marigny.
One drunk on absinth,
the other reeking of garlic;
both stained bitterly
with a soiled arrogance
set fast by ancient delusions
of triumphant grandeur
and divine will.

From Decadence to Carnival
they brawl beneath the street light,
incendiary and volatile,
brazen at the lunge
of each icy stab.

Grey Stripes and Plaid

Grey stripes consoling,
      chest to chest,
Plaid pressing pink
shuttered clapboard
against a corner house
      in the "Triangle"

Plaid pulls Stripes
'cross herringbone brick
baring down at the edge
where Saint Anthony's finished-off
      by Burgundy –
Stripes' blissful night
spews roiling back
down into the gutter

Not needing to see this,
I draw close the curtains
coveting the last siren's cries
before sunrise.

Dawn's breeze passed,
my shutters carry
the painful resurrection
of Stripes' ongoing hurl –

*(How now can I not return
to my window and marvel?)*

Plaid abashedly werves above,
aligned to a bent lamppost,
cowering in fear of reveal,
while Stripes slumps and puddles
sobbing verses of sorrow.

Blue Moon Caught Still Up

Blue, amber, and cotton swirl
puffed terra-cotta; angel pink cake.
Tarts traced with birdsong,
hacked by cables crossed,
ghosts rustling in backrooms,
muses screaming in your face.

Playing trombone to the sunrise,
drunken lampposts throwing up,
Saint Anthony's passed out on Burgundy
and the blue moon's caught still up.

Princesses twirling,
ceiling fans whirling,
Bicycle "G" pedals girlies.
Dauphine dances dizzy
with beans all a tizzy;
mornings stuck wasted at six.

Waking at four
leaves one famished by five
and starving by seven.
Working in solitude,
quiet and destitute,
lost in an up-hill battle.

But for now the ball's rolling
down cool and breezy green,
Saint Anthony's high on Burgundy
and the blue moon's caught still up.

The Water Rose

She walked
He danced
and the water rose

She slept in
He leapt for his pants
and the water rose

He burst in off of Canal
said he thought they all had gone the other way
and the water rose

She waited until the levees broke
Then booked it on her Harley
and the water rose

The boy ridin' Bitch took her home to Pine Grove
Where she married that boy
Only THEY knew each other's horrors
and the water rose

Of No Return

When the manifestation of joy
brings only sorrow
the tide rolls overhead
in a wall of murky brume,
drowning her as she clings
to the last branch of a tree
that she herself planted as a child.
she barely remembers
it's dedication,
she can't remember
it's reason.

The sadness comes thick and heavy
as her exhilarated smile
dips and sags beneath the weight
of confusion.

"How can all this be?"
she asks as the branch begins to bend,
(and break it will . . .
this much she knows)
"How will life ever again be pure?"
She fearfully ponders;
the waters continue to rise.

There will never be the peace
that once had shone brightly, naively.
The complexity of her deeds
will not release her,
her spirit drunken and drugged,
her passion dredged
from the straits of a roiled history
as the branch again creeks
as it bows lower still.

Rotting Confetti

The saddest of places seem
Always to glitter and
Feather themselves,
Quilled, quaffed in
Crimson, donning
Cloaks of gold

The sadness of being
Lost In the desert, the
Island, the tower and its
Rooftop beacon fending
Technical fliers from
Broadside crashes

The sadder the place the
Softer It's argument for
Dancing on graves,
Singing to the abyss
Pinging for reason in an
Echoless void where
Nothing remains but
Pain, confusion, and
Rotting confetti.

Good On Bad

Good people doing good things.
Good things growing from bad times.
Bad overshadowed by good
works for New Orleans these days.

What else she have?

Good cheating bad
right from the day the winds
started to blow.
Right from the moment the first water
captured the 'Ninth then all;
when it got up in everyone-else's shit . . .
. . . everywhere.

Up to this day.
This moment.
Now.

It staying there whistling softly
as a nightingale, jasmine blooming
murderously hot; "sultry" even
there still and dark against the far back wall
of our collective Southern mind.

The Impetuous Spirit

The impatience of the human spirit,
the same impetuousness that wrings
invention out of need, while also
causing us to stumble,
treading offsides,
falling over a line premature,
drawn to reaching out
to other's conclusions
without the certainty
of fact,
then left to lie down
and protect
our fragile
personal
honor.

But that is all normal
to the spirit healthy of experience
and sound of mind.
To those damaged and afflicted,
impatience is the edge
from where you'll leap,
or fall,
or where you'll push
some other innocent loved one
over
so you, in the end,
save the last shred
of true being,
existence,
never minding the weight
of limitations
of conscience.

The Fluidity of Borders (A Universe of Nomads)

dirt: disorder
debris,
chaos,
smoke swirling,
herd behavior,
a random consensus directing
the fluidity of borders.

the golden mean: balance
cut and grafted
upon the body,
three-fifths
of three-fifths,
of three-fifths,
ad infinitum;
uncompromising,
predictable,
restrictive.

light: perfection
refracted,
brilliant,
rays dancing upon the surface,
the radius of their gyrations
a choreography of joy,
contorting and molding perimeters
like mercury against air,
like water encountering oil,
like vaporous clouds in the sky,
like oxygen adrift or gusting
in an undulating universe
of nomads.

Not Here, Where To?

In the waning hours
of a two-year pandemic
and in the crumbled debris,
left in the wake,
of another hurricane,
many people I know
don't know what to do,
how to take their next step forward
when they'd rather stand exactly
where they've always been standing
but fixed and functioning,
in a manner,
as that particular place
had never been in before
—except in a vision
or a promise.

Traveling in search,
finding only more of the same,
over and over again,
promise,
disappointment,
then promise again.
Motels, hotels,
temporary rentals.
Rest area slumming,
droning on and on maddeningly,
the seatbelt digs into my side.
My neck cranes to ease
the tension in my arthritic spine.
I stare in the impotent rearview
at incoming semis
grinding to a halt
under interstate overheads;
beacons, altars, time capsules.

"Not here. Where to?"

An Absolute

There's something that snaps
in all of us when we accept, let go,
to a finite moment, a surrender,
mortality—even the notion of being wrong

When we're suddenly thrust
out of the plane
and cognitively
gasp our last breaths
when we turn just in time
to watch the car skip the curb
and nail us against
the hard stone wall of the bank building.

In cowardly preparation
we practice the point of no return
over and over
again we visualize
thousands of feet off the ground
no parachute
we are falling
and we are going to die.

An absolute.

Blissfully Off Axis

Where is the line
between hearing voices
and listening to one's thoughts?
That perceptual bridge
spanning daftness and lucidity,
separating song from dissertation;
where disturbances afflict the imagination
so that the mind must choose sides
even as the noise outside
leaks in through the cracks
of uncertainty
smudging the melody,
hushing the argument.
Setting reason a-spin
sending invention escaping
from orbits enbondaged
by earthly perils
to boundlessly float
blissfully off axis.

Coyote Wails

Strength with no power
Vision with no direction
Mission with no control
Answers with no question

Screams echoing endlessly
the noisiest chamber within;
words thrashing in cascading torrents
I can't stop them:
The words, the screams—anguishing.

Coyote wails

Fuerza sin poder
Visión sin dirección
Misión sin control
Respuestas sin preguntas

Snake Oil

A policy of truth
holding oneself witness
to one's personal facts
does not establish validation
of a social fact

I tell me
that I have spoken a lie
to another
and I'm okay with that
since I admit to fraud
I am guilty of the truth
and honest about my guilt.
I am good.

Denial and deceit dance.
Snake oil sold.
Dog whistle blows.
Tear gas explodes.
Children dream in cages.
A bible purloined.

Still they can sleep.

The code has not been broken.
A vow willfully kept.
By all means available,
disregarding data
diving Houdini style
into the deep
but with fake shackles
and chains with breakaway links,
a trick owing to illusory funding
tied to daddy's crimson purse strings.
Riding the coattails
of duplicitous pitchmen past

in an all white teflon suit

With their god on their side
they sleep soundly through the night

I told you my intentions.
Informed you of my plans.
I boasted that I can do anything I choose
and you cheered "DO IT!"
I acted the way you asked me to
and delivered nothing
but the very illusions
you requested of this stable genie
who leaked hissing and acrid,
before your very eyes,
from a flickering stage lamp
lit of the hard pressed oil
of a vaporous asp.

A Good Firm Handshake

"Look'em square in the eye
then take their hand as if it were yours."

That is the advice
my dad gave me

Don't judge,
simply take their hand

He said [his Paul Newman blue eyes expounding]

"Take their hand son,
take their hand."

The germaphobe recoils,
the contract slips before
the rendezvous is made

then to run
for the exit

who then will protect me
from you

You,
You scare me.
You, whom I don't want to touch

You, my dad
overlooked

He my ideal
left me struggling
with deciding whom
we lift;

whom we embrace
closely

It Won't Be Long Now

"There're not many of us left."
Driving slowly after turning right into the cemetery
past the groundskeeper's shed,
once a gazebo and bandstand.
He'd played cornet there with the academy's band.

We drive cautiously around the turn to the back of the property
peering across the markers with his window down,
looking for his people.
Nearly all of his family and most of his school friends,
from over nearly a century now, were there

"Hi Ray," he hails as we drive past a stone,
"Hi-ya Jane."
He goes on until we reach our family's place
against the encroaching woods
We're here to cut back the trees and vines
and scrub the stones

He kneels to take a hand brush
to the base of his grandfather's lichen covered memorial,
"It won't be long now Grampa,"
he whispered.
"Any day now."

The Light Of Two Geniuses Embraced

(for Frida and Diego)

Love's crippled embrace unable
to hold close forever that
which the minds of two so tied
may dream.

Fashioning images of vision
extending beyond mortality,
adjoining her room with his
as convalescing she lay
inventing that which might have been
       in some other life,
           in some other body.

And as light flooded in
upon them,
       both together,
           Frida and her beloved Diego,
art was produced
and life extended
beyond the years of their margins
to bring heroes upon us
as their own courageous morning
dawned upon two geniuses
dancing.

Love's Vacant Embrace

Upon a mattress of rose
pedals and thorns
the heart lies restless,
tossing, twisting
at hot knotted nightmares
filled with passions so painful
that sleep can't deny.

And, as if still in the prime
of sunlit youth
they lie barren in dreams
not to die, not to live,
awaiting the touch
that will embrace them once more.

Such is the practice
of tormented regret:
To desecrate one's soul
with a teasing glance backwards
unregarding of progress,
empty of faith.

Such is the practice
of death in degrees
to retch in the absence
of love's lofting peace.

The Secant Plane of Perpetual Quest

Lifelong pursuit,
chasing potential,
heeding watch
yet tracking forward
toward beacon blazing.

Radiating outward,
a secant plane slicing
into the emerging arc,
the sphere of one's life,
as it first enters light.

Over an expanse
the globe grows,
and turns and
rises then falls
in entropic grace
and decay

While the secant plane,
ever tilting skyward,
expands across time
and infinite space

Chasing,
       heeding,
              tracking
until it exits the orb.

Noting, youth nods
to the gleeful ascension
of perpetual quest.

Owsmo's Ouroboros

Owsmo
the outlander,
beyond institution,
dwarfing a universe,
devouring the vacuum.

Owsmo the conqueror,
taking up space,
reeling in the slack
littering the surface
the way Pollock dribbled
and stabbed,
like leftover spaghetti

or the porous asbestos tiles
cladding classrooms;
chaos cast, deeply layered
drawing in the eye
trapping all sound
capturing all light

Owsmo the vortex portal,
a cosmic inhalation
sucking life through an aperture
spewing vapors beyond
contrails evaporating
in another air
another world

"There's no better life than the world!"
Owsmo bellows then gasps
and the aperture opens
again grafting the atmosphere
insatiably bulimic left purging
decaying then devoured
an ouroboros infinitum
that's Owsmo.

Accepting a Stone

Thumb twiddling
translates as texting madly
(the modernist's plague)
isolationism personified
as an affectation, a tick,
a hole in the sand
buried and oblivious
to one who wonders beside

what did they do to deserve
all this attention of nothing?

left to adapt as water
welcomes a stone.

Blues for Tom

Hideaway to start.
White and red labeled brown bottles
rattling in black leather pockets,
as many as it took
to last the set,
to carry him through
the pain, the cruel memories,
the finesse of suffering,
lifting each phrase
to permeate the dim recesses
of the room's fragile soul.

Years later in Portland,
at an AA meeting
held in the same joint where you bartend in the afternoons
the very bar where you'd played
the night before,
and where I heard you once again after nearly a quarter
century,
we sat together drinking coffee,
recovering from what remained
and marveling at the miracle,
that it did remain,
that the blues was inclusive
and all-enveloping
and there really was nothing
in the world that compared.

R.I.P. Tom MacFarlin, a great blues guitarist.

Barry Keiner

Once I heard this boy at the piano,
an aged soul in a child's skin,
who played like Monk
of a thousand generations,
like Mingus
of ten lifetimes more.

your voicings ring,
notes singing still

and everyone
who ever heard your fingers drop,
felt it, knew it, was moved by the miracle.

you passed early on the way,
left slumped at the stop
with a satchel of sacred sounds
lost to a mythical song

you lost against the storm
of idols; expectations of a common genius
but you broke ice in a season numb
of temperament and challenge

Snow Job

I worked in a ski shop
in Beverly Hills
catering to the stars
weekend bunnies and
trust-fund shredders
living in the draught
plagued basin with
Alpian aspirations.
They'd send their point man
an hour early
to ascertain that we all knew
the importance of their upcoming arrival,
make the software hang sweet and
pretty and the workshop smell
like wax and mulled wine.

In they'd come, Jerry
Weintraub, Sonny Bono, and Nancy,
"these boots were . . ." Sinatra.
Harold Lloyd's grandson stoned
and giggling every Saturday morning spending
vast amounts of vacant inheritance
on bobbles of silk and Gore-Tex.

I waxed Sonny's skis and adjusted
his bindings before he slammed those
Solid Gold limited editions into oblivion.

Nancy came in looking for new boots
(wouldn't you know)
they had banned her from the hill
with the dogs she'd learned to drive in.
"I want boots I can drive in" she insisted.
"Can I drive in these?"
Pointing to the ladies competition pinks.
"Oh, I'm sorry," I sluffed

while cradling her perfumed Olympian feet,
"These boots were made for skiing, my dear,
and for you that's all they'll do."

Number Nine

From its hallowed place
atop my PF90 ViewSonic looking glass,
just to the left of the assembly of the Buddha
where a stupa of reliquary monument
symbolizing Buddha mind,
and laying in cautionary repose
exhibiting risky invitation,
I remove a pack of Camels
and shake-out firmly packed
Number 9 of 20.

Turning the quiver in my left hand,
as I light-up my ninth arrow,
I gaze into the mythical icon
with it's dancing girl shoulder,
surveying the palm trees and pyramids
and as the smoke swirls before my eyes
I realize that the Surgeon General
has chosen to speak from the place
just beneath the Arabian dromedary's
contented Cheshire grin.

So then what will I find
to have been passed behind
the desert walker?
(the long unattended ash
drops into my lap . . .)
Turning the pack once again
I read the words "Choice"
and "Quality"
then I smile at the broken balance,
the gray dusty cast
of Number 9's smoke,
left in it's haste to summon
rising thoughts of visions
past across the sands of time.

The Brass Ring

My dad stood
on the outside rail,
held in against gravity only
by his ever-casual arm draped
around a spiral embossed pole
until, at the same point
on each rotation,
he'd lean as far back as he could,
free arm outstretched,
first finger cocked at the ready,
to snap a steel ring
from a long-armed
mechanical tease,
then toss it back at the target
on the other side of the gazebo
and ready himself
for the next grab.

Every now and then
the young war hero
lieutenant bombardier
turned corporate golden boy
snagged the coveted brass ring
(worth a free ride for his family)
and we would all cheer
from the whirling circus wagon
on the backs of wooden animals
as the pneumatic calliope climaxed
and the sun continued to set.

Origami Man

Origami man
makes sweet potato fries
in a smart cooker gone mad,
pork chops browning,
pepper infusing the air,
his love coughs
in the distant other room.

Origami man stares
between the creases,
pours another Bombay
and muses of a terminus.

    Ends folded to become corners
    reinvented,
    edges re-canonized.
    Once gouging, stabbing,
    penetrating like amperage,
    like the ravishing
    of a dime dropped
    or of silence quartered,
    now so artfully aligned,
    tidy,
    absolute.

    Origami man folds,
    with an ivory bone
    wrought of a great tusk
    from an extinct beast
    —he himself is an extinct beast.
    Precision, repetition,
    guarantee lasting brilliance
    even as the light dims,
    Origami man lays another sheet
    of delicate paper
    on the tabula rasa before him.

Pork chops and greens,
sweet potato fries.
another martini
and another terminal crimp,
a cough from the other room,
and he quietly doubles over.

The Other Old Man

The other old man,
the one at the other end of the bar
boasted until he broke:
"As it is, I still pound it out
five or six hours every day
and I'm three years short of seventy-five.
Ha!
Me wife is more than
twenty years younger
and claims to have already
lost hold of the ghost,
and she says she's not seen it's chase
since before the pandemic;
before the ruin.
So now I'm beginning to level
at visions of Kildare in spring,
Burlington in fall.
Or (faltering),
maybe I should just hang myself,"
his blathering teetered
on his swollen lip
for a moment
then drooled
down his chin.

The other old lady
sings as she edits.
Rants as she waits,
but revels as she makes her stories
during the day
gleaning, like a spy
of the light, the ash
of promises burned
or bludgeoned.
Regardless,
it's mostly about the deadline.

The content is incidental.
She feeds herself with assignments,
filling herself with what she collects,
and rests only
when the truth
has been delivered.
She doesn't flinch nor turn.
The other old lady sleeps well at night
—every night.

Into his folded arms,
the other old man collapses,
his eyes empty, surrendering,
his lips bloodied,
forearms gashed,
the side of his face pressing
against the cool, alcohol
laced shellac of the bar.
For the first time in over a week,
he is silent.

Strange Little Woman

Strange little woman
discovering a new route
on the sidewalk
discovering and undiscovering
every possible alternative
forward or reverse
over the curb and into the street
or over the hedge and into the yards

In her third renaissance of the afternoon,
she twirls around backwards
and runs headlong
towards home.
        knit one,
                pearl one.
        knit one,
                pearl one.

Death Loiters

Death loiters
like the Travelers camped-out
on the neutral ground.

laying ambush
for some unwitting mark
who happens to pass

some random
distracted and dizzy
tourist with beads on

in August,
dazed by myopic bliss
shocked when the end nears

easy prey
for Death's casual glance
masking as benign

at the ball
thrown in celebration
of life's boundless joy.

The Way of Passage

It's often our best of friends, it seems
who show us the way of passage
through a harbor gateway
of long and lingering approach
then boorishly shut unceremoniously

Intensions like an oarsman's baulk,
tossing aside the transom's glow,
when suddenly there's no more stalling
and in an instant, the lunge makes forward
pass astern, miraculously gone

Cold curl of azure wave
risen at the ready,
engulfing the shore, the course, the horizon
suddenly washed into deep
darkness and sunken despair

"I don't know, do I?" he'd answer,
she remembered him mostly that way
before she'd slipped with the tide before he
and his rafted candor drifted on, unperturbed,
by his own temporality

Now, with the two of them gone,
we're left to float alone
upon the water's shimmering twilight
ready to serve a master's command
to return to the sea once more

Shadows Cast in Crossing

We enter in light
an unaccompanied shadow,
cast long and unfettered;
solitarily gracing
the ground upon which
each new step lays gently
the path of choice and chance,
awakening mysterious ramblings
and wanderlust's marvels.

Alone at first,
our feet pad forward;
true to no other's dream
then, absent of will
and empty of fear,
our shadow is crossed by another
and from that step forward
follow tracks backward, reflective of
companionship's presence and pace.

Rising to the surface in an ocean
of cyclic existence requires we not drift
in airs nor swift currents but steer
true to coarse, fending leisure
and fortune, such sweet siren calling
'cross water's desire
and friendship's allure.

And as we empty our hold, casting cargo astern,
our sorrows take flight and vision comes clear;
we turn from our tracks taking perspicuous notice
of an umbrageous encounter,
cast in crossing by fate,
for with only our shadows we pass,
our footprints in time are erased.

The Loneliest Man in the World

The loneliest man in the world
lies naked in sleep,
lies naked without sleep,
lies naked dreaming of sleep.

The loneliest man in the world
lies about his sins,
lies about his past,
lies about who he's sleeping with.

The loneliest man in the world
lies big lies,
little lies,
grandiose lies,
minimalist lies . . .
lying about lying around lying
about doing something,
nothing,
anything he did,
or does,
lies about lying
like it might make lying become
real.

Like lying, in the style of his mother's lies
was o.k.,
his father's lies
forgivable,
his own little white lies
justified, with an eye
toward possibilities.

A Good Plumber

Mike came over the day before he died
to reconnect a shower he had disconnected months earlier
when we reran our drain pipes.
He brought Mr. Lee with him.
Mister Lee sat in the truck while Mike worked on the shower.
After a while I asked Mike if Mr. Lee would like to come in
and hang out in the backyard near to where Mike was working.
Mike went out and ushered Mr. Lee to where I'd put out a lawn chair.
"can I get you anything Mr. Lee?" I asked.
"No I'm fine, thanks for askin'" he replied.
"You know what I could use right now Mr. Lee?" I quipped.
"I could use a Manhattan, Mr. Lee."
Mr. Lee awoke.
Mr. Lee rose out of the chair and came in close.
"Can we please have a Manhattan?" Mr. Lee begged.
When I came out with two Manhattans, one for me and one for Mr. Lee,
Mike was crawling out from under the house.
"That's that, you're good to go." Mike announced.
Mike and Mr. Lee went out drinking that night after work
and somewhere along the way
Mike had a heart attack and died.
He was only something like 52.
I often think of Mike and of Mr. Lee
and wish that they'd stop by again one day.
I'd make Manhattans.

Heart Almond Nugget

His sight rendered glacial peaks clouded in
evaporation, hazy spouts of steam rising off
melting ice, but his vision stood fast in the shifting
snow, tramped firmly into boot pressed furrows.

Drifts leaning against glazed bent bows
blanketing streambed, boulder, and barn,
still falling silently; filling the hollow as
it had in this season each year.

Heavy load holding him deeply in his tracks,
grounded upon frozen cushion levitating
over fences and onto rooftops with steps
carved by godly mission and impish jig.

And though he may shrink then expand
then shrink again, over and over,
his satchel full then empty, then full
as never before, in each turn growing greater

Than the previous pack, and as the cold breaks
against his coats, his blood pumps hotter within
his skin leathered, his heart almond nugget, his breath
glistening crystal and pure.

Raving Sick

She's raving sick
Screaming through your trailer
Breaking plates, throwing lamps

It's the CIA or FBI
Russian agents
Aliens made her

Chase you
To lock yourself in
Your car trembling

She emptied your hunter's freezer
Of two seasons' bounty
In a heap on the lawn poured

Gasoline from a bottle
Soaking thawing flesh
The stench rose as

Paranoid and confused
Drunk on jealousy
Emotionally damaged

Repeat offender
Failed over and over again
By a system confounded

By greed and corruption
And little to no interest
In her illness nor desperate plea

Egos Amok

a former lover imposing continued ownership;
publicly using a pet name past,
like the arm draped over a charge's shoulder,
the arrogant leash announcing

an assumptive gesture
labeling, objectifying, minimizing,
canceling another's freedom,
blurring one's identity.

in violation, the line defining
insecurity and self-affirmation
is erased, jilting reality,
sending egos amok.

Attack Therapy

It was one of the longest
drives of my life:
You telling of Synanon,
me hedging on my own cults;
Cambridge, Berkley,
and The Farm.

You drove the grapevine,
I, the rest.
You boasted of Mendoza
and your Argentine pedigree.
You crowed of self,
and hooted
of your achievements
at Technicolor
and the courts;

Widows and orphans,
The Troubles, and the rise.
An immigrant's struggle,
a refugee's will.

   Little left but to fend,
   to resist,
   then to hide.

   Little left—not to dig
   further, disconnected,
   inwardly derided.

You nearly ran me off the road,
called me a con artist, but spoke
as if I were a seraphim.

Synanon was rapt in discovery,
your stories told themselves—

playing The Game
on one you mistook
as nacient, naive,
and needy.

That Sneering Cross We Bear

You see that cross
you see it everywhere
that glistening corrugated cross,
factory-made panels
cleanly trimmed, formulaic
white bake-o-lite,
secular greed
superimposed
over faith, over piety;
a tin knocker's slanted vision
tossed on America's front lawn
one life gouged,
one life sated.

You see it everywhere.
Along the highway
leading someplace
where you know
you should have been
instead traveling . . .

Some places demand due
while some things, and places
do more

Placing wealth
where money never mattered.
Perfectly creased miters
pointing skywards
while the world below
sneers

That intersection
splitting hell
from everything else
means nothing

to those driving past
that prefabricated scythe
they'd never live
to sling.

The Philanderer's Daughter

Oh, how you should have
Been there to end it, to
Smite my hand and
Slap the clarion
Horn from my lips

Arrogance, piousness your
Spirit lamenting,
Abandonment, sorrow in
Aspic gelling
Fear and dolor into
Paddies of repulsion,
Remorse and refusal, he

Bruised you at his table
Starved you when you hungered
Loved you beneath his wing but
Trashed you before the Pope, the

Almighty Canon, the
Slanderer, the thief, the
Philanderer, your father,
Abuser divine, who

Art now in heaven as
Have you these last
Sixteen years, when
Without him, you ran
Amok, 'less your ernest and
Noblest intentions

Quickly getting tossed out of
Wellesley for baring your
Soul and your breasts
Skinny dipping in Lake Waban
Not because it was hot but that his

Heart ran cold, so
Mercilessly frigid

Practicing acceptance, the
Bar boisterously singing
Ancient Viking melodies while you
Drafted your escape in
Lock-keyed diary so
Whenever, you'd be ready to
Sail back to Sweden

Fearful of the poison passed
Wildly at the rail's end, you
Sipped wine through a straw, spat
Daggers of mistrust, rued
Nothing since your expulsion

Ancestors turning upon their
Son, disingenuous the monster
Who locked you out, but they
Side with you now, from their
Norseman's stony graves,
Out to you reaching with

Gnarled fingers, punctured arms
Spinning in air like ribbon candy
Sweet lilting filigree, fragile
Ready to shatter at any
Moment fallen

Oh, had you been there
Tonight as the priest called
Out for all, to witness, his
Lost letters of promise, you

Must have been tossing
'Neath the weight of your
Broken bones—having
Never been able to

Save the child
Torn from your youth
Swaddled in hate so
Chillingly buried

Missing what had never been
Echoing now against the
Vaulted sanctum
Exploding upon an
Altar of hypocrisy, your
Legacy regrettably
Trounced in the missive; your
Unquieted absence.

The Preacher's Stained Cup

in spirit's wrap shredding
stuffed into a pillowcase
charred but never completely burned
stashed forever

behind the altar at St John's,
heavy as eternity it remains
the hole bored
through Pius' prayer maniacal

a ghost's blathering alibi
a gap left spurting
vial contempt for angels
fear of truths proven

and burdens leased usufructo
to innocents plying forgiveness
and willing to pay their week's wages
just to kiss the ring

tagging the past they never had
with a future they'd never know
running willy-nilly still
'cross obstacles planted

by god-fearing preachers
in cardboard vestments
wrenching glittering gibberish
from tin foil pulpits

the mark stretches past
one life, two . . . countless more
it rumbles on echoing
hate begetting contempt

pissing insecurity into an open palm of generosity

dripping down between open fingers
too gripped at the collection tray
to save even a single drop

Eight or Nine Times

"Eight or nine times,"
said she,
"eight or nine times outta ten."
She knew this to be
statistically true because
she was a teacher
of children of "that" age.
Still, she was young
and new to teaching;
she was still an idealist.

"Those children scare me,"
said he,
"they loud; sayin' things
I never heard my momma's
children say. One day
I fear one of them's gonna kill me."

"No, no – that's not so,"
        said she,
"They're not all bad
like that,
As a matter of fact,
probably eight or nine
outta ten wouldn't
kill you at all."

Vanilla

vanilla with chocolate eyebrows
like ribbon candy
incandescent in the room
behind the kitchen

crystalline jazz and rock noir
cassettes clicking at their end
then whirring into rewind
and auto-repeat all afternoon

a basket of others
spent and unspooled
a nest of songbirds grounded
on the cold board floor

to wobbling fan paddles
strobing we pour
and count cobs coursing
on ceiling convections

sugary lace
on linen and tat
riffing off a jug
and wasa bread with butter

cucumbers, gravlax
and Akvavit sprinkled
upon a starched collar stained
bloodied tourniquet of the mind

Tin Can Tiara

Wearing a tin can tiara
and a teacup glance
she rolls out the chocolate
with queenly vision and verve.

Mab in silver shackles
rattling verse of whispered flight
and pending adventure,
        dancing light,
glimmering thought,
she recites from Dante and Keats.

Another "gangsta" she ignites
smoke rising toward Napoleon's ceiling,
"He built this place," she explains,
"but he never made the crossing
to see it himself
so now I park my Harley
in the emperor's carriage-way
and rave at my royal fortune."

They come to her in cavalcade
of art and inspiration,
voices raised, piano keys caressed
and trombones wailing in the night.

She pours tea to Englishmen
coffee to gamesmen and thieves,
fresh milk, she sets out
for the stray calico
that haunts the shadowed alley.

And when the sun shows clearly
and the breeze gently shines,
she kick-starts her steed,
riding over dream swept streets
in her gilded tapestry's spree.

I.C.U. Salsa

I.C.U. Salsa,
sort of an emergency room for the soul,
where you check yourself in
while I'm out of town.

The doctors there treat you
with the clave's infusion
of relentless repetition,
they bandage your repressed bliss,
masking the hurt
with clattered distraction.

Like the rattle of the old
unbalanced ceiling fan
overhead in this hotel lobby bar
blurs the silence of distance
as does the sloshing of ice-cubes
in my umpteenth drink.

Shoving off to slumber,
sailing away from muddied banks,
a shore toxic with jealousy
and flooded with fear,
I see you salsa in dark
uneasy dream.

The Window

She sits by the window
in the evening
as the sun goes down,
as the neighbor's dog
barks to be let in
as the tide of traffic
on the next block
drifts into waves of crickets
buzzing out back
beyond the garden.

She sits by the window
and sees her children walking
up the middle of the street,
returning with a flag
and a can,
and newspaper rain hats;
barefoot and laughing
splashing through puddles
beneath bug clouded street lamps
and firefly star light.

She sits by the window
with the radio playing softly.
Night after night,
weeping.

She Lifts

she lifts the rubbish
off the Esplanade neutral ground
(one hand trash)
while her dog sniffs the curb,
     (the other hand leash)
shopping for somewhere to squat,
a place appearing perilous
on the very edge of the street
where passing drivers, thinking
they might waste a dog at his stool,
give break-light to panic
and symphony to action.

go-cups and candy wrappers,
unopened condoms, diapers,
and chicken wing bones . . .
all lifted upward, back into the air;
nested gently as one
in a re-born plastic Schwegman's bag.

sometimes he uses the monkey grass
where deep in dark thicket
the invisible lays undone;
sometimes he goes on the newly mown lawn
and finishes by kicking hard to his rear
tearing St. Augustine up by the root
in a mixed-bag of shrapnel,
bark, cinders, urban debris,
blasting car doors and rolled-down
driver's side windows.

she places her bags carefully
in the dumpster on the corner
then turns and smiles at her trash-less course,
"others will follow in step," she whispers
then strides off down the street

Saint Anthony's Book of Psalms

Thirty-nine years before
yesterday's Valentine's Day
a hole opened in the sky
and the floor fell away
in a moment suspended
between the festering rot
of failure
and the blossoming pedals
of promise

It had been seven years before that,
struggling to cultivate a harvest
of trust.
Tilling, planting,
tending, picking
yet a yield so scant
hunger nested in
the wintry rafters
to perish before the thaw.

Over the frozen crest,
down the sunny side sliding,
crystalline onset melting
through fourteen more years
until the splintering floor
washed into the gulf and,
again, the sky
spun wildly ajar.

Valentine's granddaughter,
hanging-in for twenty-five tomorrow,
wears a Saint Anthony medal,
searches the sidewalks
and neutral grounds
for lost locks
and discarded keys,

sweetly gracing the damned
and cradling the forlorn
with her loving gaze.

Thirty-nine years recovered
in a blink, then burned,
to the sound of trombones cooing
in golden light dancing.
Jasmine and oleander,
magnolia perfume,
pollen lilting in suspension
exorcizing shadowy threats
with fragrant adventure
that wafts in the evening's return
like Anthony's book of psalms
miraculously drifting home to Padua.

He Couldn't Remember His Wife Had Died

He couldn't remember that his wife had died.
Alone, he fumbled with the coffee maker,
Not sure where she'd kept the beans, the grinder.

Calling up the back stairs, he waited, pretending
that her voice would echo down through the bead-board stairwell
but he knew, or at least had a hunch,

that she could no longer hear him.
He paused and listened as hard as he could
but her words would not be coaxed.

Clumsily lifting a paper filter up to the ceiling light,
he smiled at the silhouette of his enfeebled fingers behind it,
then sank gently into her chair at the grey Formica table.

White Gravy Boys

(For Arnold Gerber)

Chunky Davis said to Barn Hill:
"Ya'll gotta git back down inta'dat hole an' weld!"
you my, 'white gravy boys'."

We'd wrap these white blankets around us
(they was all asbestos)
an' we could weld all day long
and never get burned,
galvanized by the green smoke
in the hold.

Chunky later died of a brain hemorrhage
from having his head kicked-in by Barn Hill

Then there was Heavy Evans,
now there was one mean sonofabitch.

The Warped Road to Home

It begins with dominating the social setting
often through a sequence of stories grand to begin
then becoming grander with each recurring slur
rolling steadily downward toward some public demonstration
defiant of connection, urgent with command.

At first it would mercilessly floor me –
my jaw fisting beneath my ears,
my spirit sagging past my heels –
flagging angrily I'd likely err in word or gesture,
or both before bolting out the room to brood
alone slouching beneath the rear-view
until she swaggering in song
slaps her hand down on the dashboard,
glows inward with eyes and smile to the heavens
before turning the key
for the long and vacant,
warped ride home.

Now my jaw, unyielding,
leads me out the door
with the first uttered:
"I wuth photographing thizguy today when . . ."
The touch of toad upon princess wasted.
Alas.

Of such night I'm now recovering.
Things are somewhat normalized
as we pass with off-turned eyes.
"I hope you're writing all this down," and
"differences are accentuated these days."

Haunting thought-bytes echo determined,
I will prevail. She singing country
readying to run out
and shoot a big fire in Gentilly.

It was somewhere between
the produce section and the shrimp
that her cell rang:
"new york times, they want the fire."
"Is it still burning?" I ask.
"Guess so but I kinda' doubt it."

We finish with the groceries,
crash the bags into the kitchen
and then she splits again.

Inside Out

(for Don Rose)

The pedals of a rose
long ago swept away
by the current of the Charles
now rise, in a moment's tide,
so fragile and perfect
as they never had been in life.

We met in the middle of the bridge
to scatter your ashes over the water's surface
and spend our thoughts together
as an adopted family of misfits
that you tailored as proxy
for blood lost over anger,
misunderstanding, and rejection.

You died a burn victim,
not by the flame or smoke
of an external fire
but from a catastrophic reaction
to the drug AZT,
it was to be your miracle
but now it left you burning
from the inside out.
Flesh blistered in rage
because it had many times
known a soft caress
but yearned, unfulfilled,
to be caressed with true love.
In the end, it was morphine.
"Give me more," you screamed, "I can't take
this pain any longer.
Please, if there's a God,
give me all the morphine you have."
And the night nurse complied
as we stood at your bedside

This morning I unpacked a box
of books that you had willed to me.
Biographies of great composers,
libretti of operas you loved so dearly,
and there, pressed between the pages
of a documentary study of Mahler,
should I come upon two
beautifully preserved cannabis leaves.

I lift the leaves from the pages,
crumble them together
and place them in a common bowl.
The smoke swirls into my lungs
and then, in exhalation,
gently rises in fractal twine.

Seven Doors

It was always more
about the hang,
friends lingering to
pass a joint and

sate that gnawing need,
to find balance,
amid distraction
and social din.

Composing a sound-
track that eases
pain through a gauntlet
emotional.

Filtering out doubt,
trepidation,
through a screen built of
ivy and verse.

Like a mid-century
barbershop's buzz,
with its doors awide,
joy clamoring.

Passing apple wine
and idle steps
toward love's whim and fate.
Smoke rills upward

carving it's way through
time and tempers,
lifting the circle,
billowing high.

    At ten or fifteen bucks a lid

No one went hungry
No one left feeling alone

I never took drug tests,
I've always smoked pot
But today I peed
In a cup for its prescription,
so to pay tax on the muse.

The elevator doors opened
directly into the waiting room
The intake nurse pointed to
the restroom door and
handed me a vile

I obliged and returned
to be ushered to
a door numbered three.
It opened into an exam
room. I waited.

Door number four
opened to a lobby
with another intake nurse
and this time a cop

My license, birthdate, address
confirmed
hands me ticket B26 and
buzzes me in through
door number five

My license, my birthdate, my address
confirmed
through door number six then
door number seven,
the third on the right.

I take a chair

I place my order,
flower and vape,
pay with plastic then
exit back into the light,
bag in hand walking
through the parking lot
just like leaving Walgreens

No banter
No news
No pirate stories
No apple wine
No pipe passing
No joy clamoring
No ivy of verse
No love's whim
    nor fate.

A Perfectly Pressed Leaf

The perfectly pressed leaf
You left between
Page '49 and 1990
Fell out today
Brittle now
after all these years

Fragile truths whisper
In incidental forms
Left hidden and wilting
In slow, dusty graduations
From where one plays
To . . . well, where
We visited your bedside

You closed
the coffee table tome
Shelved it with the rest
Then crawled between
Drenched sheets
Shivering

Your chaos became
our routine reliable
In casual pace and practice
Until indifference
Left you unattended
To die alone, of your own
Morphine hand

Then, deep
in the darkness of time's
Passage you leapt
From the pages
As an unwitting stranger
Selected an attractive perusal,

Flexed its spine
As you floated
finally free.

The Still Warm Soil of Evening

A flower bent
at its stem, injured

Wind marching
to a sky beaten drum

Midday sun careening
past the promise of dawn

Petals drop
from the corolla parched

Beauty left barren
In the still warm soil of evening

Wilting Lotusland

As the cool reptilian night
slips beneath the sunrise
in a dark and wilting Lotusland
the heat of a swampish hell
swells into another day
of stinking rot and vomit,
sidewalks stained greasy
from kitchen fat and urine
tracked across the Quarter
by tourists wearing flip-flops
and rolling coolers full of cheap beer

Blue Carpenter Bee

I followed her
from the garden
across the lawn
and through the thicket
to the dock

the sun-warmed boards
were old and soft,
she waited there.
until I caught up,
drawing near

to where she set,
disturbed, she took
off again on
air, over the still
canal; gone.

Slapstick Sickos

Pulling to
load-down vixen
fading through bad,
hard and nasty
slapstick sickos.

Hot cat song
raging up
from beneath the house,
banging pipes,
knocking wood scraps,
clatter and crack,
on the dash
out from under.

Distracted and flaccid,
I retreat to
pour more concrete.

Frogs Slinging Pearls to Trombones

Frogs croak to each other in the backyard
while the murder rate in New Orleans rises once more
after a hiatus served from an imported cop
now the frogs call in others from where only
the frog god knows.

And accordions squeeze on the gallery
along side a trombone squealing through the plunger
and a slide guitar with knotted strings.
Cell phones marry precocious PDAs
over azure martinis and picador olives.

"She called to tell me you were here playing saxophone tonight"
he said as I joined them at their table
"how was I to know?"
she countered as to say "it doesn't really matter, does it?"

Well it does, damn it. It's important to me
and I'll be damned if I don't set her straight.

"Listen," I say. "Saxophones are like toads,
what I play roars like those bull frogs out there,
calling in their betrothed, lying in wait
to string eggs; laced pearls
that I will scoop out of the pond in the morning
after you've gone back to your uptown flat
to listen to tangos played by some dead Argentine fiddler.

The Nihilist Wind

When liquid drizzles then dries;
when light fades to darkness,
and sound is muted in silent terminus;
will, in this end, the story yet be told?
Will time grace the future
as it has caressed the past?
Will the present survive?

Or, as dust disperses
in a nihilist wind
and candle-light suffocates
in a nescient vacuum;
will an idiot din
drown time's sentient song
and cast it forever unsung with no voice
with which to court its own self?

Either way,
what difference will it make
if time itself were to become frozen
with fear and denial?

The state in which we rest
serves no more, nor less,
than the service we leave undone.
Still, in the present, we can sleep,
indifferent to the trappings of the moment
as the pain of evidential circumstance
pales compared to options of fear or complacency
haunting life in a causal reality.

Each moment witnessed is dwarfed
by our inability to focus absolutely
upon that which dangles infinite
or flails amorphic.
No fence, no interior;

form without line being formless,
or so it must appear to the fearfully unimaginative.

And in the rattle of such little noises,
the creative soul is lost to disturbance and pain,
sinking in an uncontrolled, spiraling plummet
toward the hard-deck of fathomless depression.

Turning phrases or turning pages,
spinning tales in ostinati differs little
from being locked in a procrastinational cycle
of masturbation.
Rising and falling
over and over again
to manically conjure the invention
of non-repeating climaxes.
New only at the moment of apogee.
Unique only in our blind-sided arrogance
causing them to linger stubbornly
in our caressing hand.
We choke the ego
till it gasps then sputters,
wringing utterance from stoned absence
then coax spew from a sputter.

We insist upon genius
each time our tragic corps falls
yet roll over and fain sleep
once our muse again rises.

Angry Typing

Angry typing
tapping hard . . .
no, punching keys
in an angst driven
fire storm
of impatience and
frustration.

Vein popping palms
wrenching at
reddening brow

"Shit!"
(backspace)

pound's first into desk
against interruptive ringing
of phone AND head

"Damn it!"
(backspace, delete)

fingers to mouth
gnawed nails
to recessive nubs.

The pain of panic
bloodied pallet
wasted toil and
squandered solace

"Shit! Shit! Shit!"
(backspace, backspace, backspace)

slams her office door
cursing knob, hinge, and latch

trapping herself in
a hot-box
wrought with fear
and warmed by failure

(backspace, delete, escape)

Cardboard Convictions

Cardboard convictions
In corrugated vows

Parceled regrets
Sealed tight of excess

A tape redacted past
Inked in black pentel stripes

The same familiar drop-point
Metered burden, post pre-paid

The carrier's van
Destinational promise

Transited dreams
Shipped next day air

Unhanded delivery
Left stranded at the door

Then secreted off
As it's heisted by shadows

Box knife gashed label
Binding twine slashed

To another revealed
The tragedy unwrapped

Dispatched of pain
Ratcheted no more

Shards strewn in scatters
Of shivers dismembered

La Polilla Perdida

la polilla perdida,
la llama baliza

parpadeando, dibujando la lente
sobre la frágil luz

flota por un momento
la captura es rápida

en ala a la deriva
lavado de musa a capricho

ella aterriza agotada
sobre la flor silvestre del amor

hasta una propensión exigente
abruma el descanso del momento

The Lost Moth

the lost moth,
the beacon flame

flickering, drawing the lens
upon such fragile light

a moment fleet
the capture swift

on wing adrift
flushing muse to whim

she lights, depleted,
upon love's sylvan blossom

an exigent propensity
overwhelming the moment's rest

Piss Flies

The piss flies
flew over from the stables.
They flew straight toward it.

The odor.

The stench swirling upward
was traced
in their approach
as they were suddenly diverted,
rising in vectors.

in circles,
ascending
then momentarily fall
airless and weak;
befuddled
for a moment
then inspired,
their passion rekindled,
as a draft,
hurling them skyward,
revives their urgency
to reach the death
of another
lying in the garden
beneath the mint
and garlic chives.

Each, in turn,
with the renewed verve
from the muses of the winds,
dives intently toward the carcass,
strafing it with imaginary,
anticipatory forks brandished.
Nothing else mattering.

Nothing else visible.
Now they belong to the meal,
the meal they have not yet alit to.

A gusting perturbation,
rough air indiscriminate,
leveler of fate,
jerk of nature,
claps . . .
. . . and they are
unceremoniously tossed
from the table,
expelled back to the heavens
where they will awake
(not knowing what the hell just happened)
hungry.

And with a deliciously scented hangover,
they once more smell promise
in the herb patch
on the ground
at the end
of a sweetly acrid fume
rendering present against past,
and so once again
they piss
their brief lives
away.

I woke with a start at 1:23
so I turned on the overnight news
but dozed off before the second story.

When I next came to,
the blurry LED on the night stand read 2:34
just in time to watch the replay of the second news story
then drop back off to sleep

Until I rolled to my side and crushed my glasses
into my cheek thus waking me again; 3:45!
I finish the overnight broadcast
and watch the continuing replay of the first story
before nodding off again.

At exactly 4:56
the TV timed out and the sudden silence
jolted me back to consciousness.
I rose out of bed fearing that,
if not and I were to fall back to sleep,
I might next awake to the clock reading 5:67
and that scared the hell out of me.

Tres Besos (Eating Tacos)

The greeting:
    two old friends collide
        rhapsodically chanced
           thrilling

The embrace:
    they dance upon the table
        blissfully conjoined
           relishing

The farewell:
    their inevitable parting
        a last remnant taste
           pining

Lost All Interest in Cooking

Life is a four-letter word
But so is alas

I lust for my wife like she's twenty-three
She reminds me we've traveled far

Children, some close, some distant
some raising families, some racing carts

The beach we lay upon eroding with each wave's wash,
though grappling inland is entangled with discontent

Tyrolean dreams fade in northward retreat
as our sagging balloon drifts reluctantly toward Mexico

Seems every time I refurbish a kitchen
we sell and move out of the house

I've finished another kitchen
I've now lost all interest in cooking

Fifty Sense

Of the ringing in my ears
and the blurring in my eyes,
distortion begets a burgeoning
new order out of the fading familiar.

Like when, as a child,
I'd twirl until dizzy
then fall beneath
the magical spinning sky;
reeling in revelation,
giddy with discovery
knowing safety
as an adventure
into the self-
contrived mysterium
of physiological manipulation.

Now, in bending grace,
my dilutions wash
over me in trickling failure.
As tissue melts in entropy
the wonder of chaos becomes
a horror of confusion;
swirling reads its own moment
without regard to fancy,
and madness replaces whimsy
uncaring of experience,
oblivious to dream.

When All Our Rescues Have Gone

Runaways,
refugees,
we rescued them all,
my wife and I,
timidly cracking the door
only to toss it wide open
a lineage passing over our doorstep,
years of fostering
person or pet.
A nephew suffering
of an ill mother.
A stray Labrador retriever
who showed up on Mardi Gras morning
and never left.

There were only two remaining,
then the boy went away last year
now it's just the dog
and us.

Tonight, the dog
is in the hospital
and we're wondering
what it will be like.

Etched in a Time of Reckoning

I used to burn through journals like mad
One or two pages upfront
Then time and distraction rendered
Pages, the balance remaining, blank
Unscathed and barren of woe
Book after book of bounded whiteness
With only initial scratchings
Scrawled in moments of emptiness
Themselves a vacant tabula
Musings that had to be freed
Thoughts that would eventually alter
Our trajectory and posture to
Send the spacecraft homeward
And crash on camera but reveal nothing
This box of binders and dust covers
Lost in the pain of memories
Etched in a time of reckoning.

Wasn't Always Like This

Wasn't always like this;
surrounded dark under single lamp,
wrapped in technology:
racks, lights, mixers, controllers.
This ancient attic view up Burgundy St.
shuttered, sealed, and baffled with only an old photo
of Satchmo beaming, dangling from a nail in the ceiling.
Could be night or could be day;
temperature tight and acoustically insulated,
silent save the blow of the furnace
and the rumbling earth beneath wheels of haulers
and cherry pickers rising early
to fix this mashed-up city;
this bread-pudding sliver of sediment we float upon
thunders under the weight of their charge
causing all on deck to move and resound from down deep;
a roaring yawn, shaking bones at rest to animate.

It's four a.m. when she clicks off the TV racket
and I'm jolted awake and ruminating;
rehashing what I'm supposed to do,
what it is that I'm supposed to do,
why I'm going to do it, or
how I'm going to get out of doing it.
The tube quiets my mind,
demands my focus and keeps my circuits from crossing
through a carefully orchestrated matrix of ordered din
playing just loud enough over my thoughts
to comb away all snarling synapses amuck.
Without it now I spin, toss, and fumble
unable to find my glasses on the first try
and knocking something loud to the floor.
I hit the trifocal on the second-try by the light-stand
and sweats now from (likely) layers down into the hamper
but that's soft and safe in the dark
when someone else is trying to sleep

and I retrieve them instantly
knowing their drawstring right off
then creep soft closing the door
to the stairwell and aerial glow,
I pad upward.

The Dark Phantasmal Night

The self-indulgence
of practicing an instrument
when one has no gigs
can easily sting villainous.

"What'd you do today?"
"I played trombone,
alone,
at home."

The punchline echoes
as reason shakes its head.

Long tones breathing circular
Across the fullest blue range
From whispering shadows
To exploding fits
Of stentorian thunder.
Scaling hillsides
Beneath arpeggiated skies
Raining both hot and cold
From a twelve-foot funnel cloud.

It gnaws deeply,
the guilt, the self-loathing
—never finding forgiveness,
demanding either immediate action
or dismissive acquiescence;
submitting to futility
(still ringing villainous)
remorseful surrender,
left empty of fight,
to eventually slip back off
and into the lap
of the dark
phantasmal night.

Afar from the Din of Despair

Life in New Orleans' Marigny,
party and Airbnb central filled
with abhorrent human noise
mixed with the grinding
electro-mechanical drones,
buzzes, and hammering
of the objects, devices,
and the total of all delirious
plenum produced by humans.

Deprived, classist, desperation,
the locals' manic run repulsive
to exposition and self-affirmation,
the desperate urgency of tourists,
transplants, and hipster interlopers—ruthless
wannabes and endowed heirs
of America's most fashionable
and arty elite—leaves me cowering
in the silence left behind,
in the back streets of the Faubourg
cars beached on the neutral grounds,
blocking indefensible driveways,
they sashay down to Decatur Street
to scream for trinkets and guzzle
all the moonlight they can steal.

I draw a bath, pour a glass
of Bordeaux, and whisper
dreams of no more theist rituals
—the obvious and predictable,
splashing in celebration of love
not power, not prosperity,
nor repression, with its
shameless opportunity.

There's an element of the city's culture

that has become pathetically reliant
upon rhapsodical adulation of
a caricatural dilettantism.
The local axiom:
"If you can't make it here don't leave,"
feeds into a doomed ouroborosic cycle
of banal repetition and predictability
upon which its primary industry,
tourism, has come to rely:
Emulators of old-timey jazz,
purveyors of imitation cookery,
dancers of appropriated exotic steps
spilling everywhere into the trenches furrowed
by lost generations now chased asunder
by wealth and naive opportunism.

But as the circus delirium
rapes the mind, shoving proud fists
of self-acclaimed pap
into the Lower Quarter
and Upper Ninth,
I slide released into my tub
to bathe in steamy silence
and blissful reflection
only found when the petulant parade
rolls off in distant, faraway places.

Another Limp Martini

Two fantails introduced
to two paws dipping,
lunging at liquid,

fluid swimmers unwary;

grasping with toes spread wide,
claws fully spent,
empty splashing only

I reach further with two fingers
      splayed,
           deeper,
                fruitlessly,
                     thirsty . . .

Again the goldfish swim by.

Into the jar, swirling brine
loosening but one pimento
free as flotsam

I pour another limp martini.

Blackness First

Blackness
first as I close my eyes
and slip deeply into dark's embrace.
Strata by strata more comforting,
each level cradling me
more gently than the last.
The light locked out
with its brutish indifference
while tight inside: Nothing but bliss.
Warmly wrapped.
Swaddled in blackness.
Blackness consoling.
Blackness protecting.

The blaring noise of parched earth.
Bleached sand so hot to the eye
it sees a shoreline levitate
above the desert floor.
An armada passes.
Sailing ships tossing.
Saint Elmo's Fire crackling;
white sparks raining down
on sleeping victims below.
White lightning.
White noise.
White powders racing.
Whiteness killing precious time.
Whiteness erasing life.
Whiteness threatening.

Blackness remaining,
calm and present.
Always, blackness remaining.
Blackness being there
long before, longer after,
always securing the last word.

Whiteness hovering around
waiting for every opportunity
to prank and cheat the moment
with glaring contempt
for those who dwell
in the cool sheltering shade of
blackness.

Fear and Proximity (Boundaries in Air)

separate   souls bowing,
    acquiescing
but   only together in open
    embrace,
equal   to less when left alone,
    each one pulling for the greater

good   we ponder the paradox
    that things taken place behind
fences   may never really have happened

    if gone completely unwitnessed. So, we
make
    excuses and pretend to be
good
    while all along being nothing but bad
neighbors   griping about the dog next door
    incessantly yapping at our cat
    sleeping on the wall between us.

not
    blending, cloistering
in
    -stead developing
my   -opic views; intolerance
    passed to our children with
back   -ward teachings
                        in the temple and the school
yard   brawling in the sand
    over boundaries in air.

Spilt Milk

*(For London Thomas, her father, and all victims of the mass shooting at
the Tops Market in Buffalo NY 5/15/2022)*

He was shooting at the milk,
    baby.

He was just shooting at the milk
    Not us
    Not those who are us
    Not those who look like us

Not to kill you
    or me
        or your gramma
            or your auntie

The parental lies of reason
protecting, for the moment,
the putting off of understanding
until understanding becomes attainable

But there is no attaining
the rationale of hate

There is no attaining
the coward's mind

Swaddled in the sheltering arms
of her father
huddled on the floor
against the dairy case,
the gun shots raged
the gallons of milk bled
her heart dropped

His honor feeling the impact

His ancestors screaming
His heirs retching
His arms embracing
an unimaginable survival

And the milk gushing, bleeding,
flooding the aisle of
the only source of groceries
within reach
a Tops at the bottom
of her food chain

Her food oasis
Her community needing,
Her needing this for life,
Her needing this place like
a tabernacle of recognition
and sustenance
in a world already cemented
in jealousy and animosity.

The intercom continues oozing
pre-programmed string tracks
and the checkout lines realign

On and on
Just another blip
One more skip of faith
In the end,
one will right the boat
swamped by unknowingness;
the crags of cowardice,
that lurk below the surface,
truth replaced by hate.

White, Tree Line, Black

All up in there they were
up there in Jena,
up there hanging in the tree
hanging in the morning
just to show how dark the night was,
how dark it might be again,
dark youthful ignorance
shrouded by the delusion of a silence
their parents uncomfortably keep;
made tame, commonplace
as an elbow's errant surge
or a leg's covert thrust
'twixt pride and panic,
laying ambush in path
as fear mires a moat,
they shelter their children
from what they themselves don't understand,
from what they're most afraid of.

White, tree line, black
line painted elegantly mapped,
aligned perfectly with where
the white tree once stood.
Stump-ground white tree missing
so quick, before more can come,
like deep in the sand, hidden from sight
but stinking to the taste so putrid
to chase memory asunder and fade.

Nooses tied by junior rodeo clowns
just to show them, to hang, to die
at the end of a rope . . .
. . . to make them imagine what it means
to hang from a tree by a rope tied by a white man,
a white man that you know,
a white man who has said before, many times

that he likes you, that he respects you,
that he admires you
but has never sat with you beneath his tree
nor under yours.

First a respectful address
of a dubious practice
and request for permission
to ignore the folly
of a socially out-of-step tradition
is dismissed by principle as "jocular."
then nooses neatly knotted by dawn
dangle in "jocular" retort;
from this, one must run
or prepare to fight
to the death fore death become
the substance and circumstance
of Hatred's icon,
but the DA cites innocence of youth
while pointing deadly intent as an adult,
getting victim and perpetrator
conveniently crossed.

Stupid isn't perceptual. Stupid is self-defining.
Stupid can be naive and stupid can be blind
but stupid can never be taken back
and stupid can only add to the suffering,
it is stupidity alone that explains the jailing
of six black Jena Louisiana high school students
for ganging up and acting out
against the white rodeo clowns
who hung the nooses
and spent only three days in study hall
as "just and fair" punishment.

Stupidity and stupidity alone
accounts for the pain suffered by a community,
each individual citizen, in their own way,
broken by stupidity,

the kind of stupidity lurking deep
in the thick piney woods
of central Louisiana in 2007.

Light On the Water

Minds clashing, heads crashing
Hearts bleeding all over the place
From the inside out constructing,
walls to keep them out,
then hurling a wrecking ball
against the walls we built
to make us safe within;
amongst ourselves
here and now.

We quarrel as always
but when you threw
that stolen shield
breaking ancient glass,
a part of all that there is left
of authenticity;
Americana if it ever existed,
you pissed away your rights
in a violent denunciation,
an insurrectional tantrum,
and you lost all dignity
in the eyes of our society.
Now you sit abandoned.

The tide always rises
to fall each time
in swirls revealing
dregs and hidden dangers

High tides o'er hidden dangers
deep beneath our keel
may we glide past a fate
breathless and alone,
may we slip off to someplace
a little more demure
and in love, my dear,

and drift reflecting
in time with the flickering
light on the water.

Mariachi Insurrection

It's a Mariachi insurrection,
a red neon flashing
sombrero billboard,
chasing down cars
on Eje Central Lazaro Cardenas,
waving trumpetas
and swollen guitarrons
and screaming "La Bamba"
to touristas sloshing
60 peso margaritas.

Like a swarm
of killer wanna-bees
on a merciless conquering march
they rage out of the Plaza
and into traffic,
encircling head lights,
blocking out the sky,
stinging in brassy thirds
and twisted violin unisons.

Taco stand Toreadors
choke sidewalks and alleys
and waist coated stallions
stomp in the dusty gutter
to the bellows of a Senora
with tattooed eyebrows
and a filigreed breast plate . . .

the smoke swirls beneath
blue and green tarpaulins,
strung from lamp posts
to windowsills,
eyes burn
  ears ring
    and heads spin

as a mini-van full of rancheros
pulls up to the curb,
spilling shots of tequila from the roof
and dancing upon the hood.

Then off they race
to Xolchimilco
where they crash their boat
into the Mexican moon light
and laugh insanely,
rocking the driver overboard,
and sinking their cares
beneath flowery flotsam
to be buried deep
in the drunken silt
at the bottom
of rapture's canal.

Valor's Honor

Valor's honor mustered
Soldiering truth unadorned
Sounding out facts
Where knowns are scorned

Masked of superstition
Practice, tradition, and fate
Lies in darkness
Urgency waits

To spill, as if random,
A purposeful collection
For this moment,
Time's correction

When threads come unraveled
Roads buckle, wind, and end dead
Where chalk lines fade
Scuffed smears of red

Pale and blue unfurling
The warrior bows in despair
Orders sluffed off
Hope lost to air.

Soldier of Knock

"I'm not afraid of dying,
I am afraid of losing.

They give me food and ammo,
and a place for me to sleep."

Soldier of knock,
gun in hand.

Simple as fate,
true as sand.

Americana

In this country,
on this continent,
and of this world
there has never been a lack of *stuff*
with which to justify our consequence.
But the physical stuff is but incidental
to the transient nature of our ephemerality.
The most salient measure of
our mark can be witnessed
not so much in
the material of our droppings
as in the pattern of our tracks.

With profound mission
we came to this place,
myopic in our urgency
to escape our past
and become Americans. But
as we now yearn to look back,
to reminisce on our heritage,
we can no longer find much
of that which has been brashly discarded
behind a forgotten horizon.

What once we considered with the grace
and grandeur of our *Manifest Destiny*
we may now be holding desperately fast to
as but a perquisite of the job;
psalms of the damned
none the better, none the less.
It's the rule not the exception:
this badge and this book,
this codification of popular consent,
this social acceptability.
These trappings of a
Euro-, Afro-, Asian, and Latino heritage

that form this muck that we stir,
be it art,
be it *pop*,
be it cultural debris,
it's ours undeniably: *Americana.*

We sailed to these shores lugging
sea chests filled with essentials:
trinkets and tools
and our ancestral scrolls;
our desiderative plenum.
We traded these things for
all we ever dreamed of and, since
we dreamed of more
than we could ever have,
we bartered beyond our means and into
a soup of chartered heterogeneity.

As we shed the derma of our past,
we donned the new skin of
an acquisitioned persona.
We didn't grow it, we grafted it.
It suited our whim so we took it
for our own then we strutted, unabashed,
before the world as if we had inherited
the divine right of kings.
But it was from a king's tyranny
that many of us had fled,
coming to this land.
Had we but run from where we were headed?
Like the nagging pull of an undertow,
the gravity of our alien heritages
would never release us to tread
unconditionally
upon the soil of this new world.

And as for those we uprooted:
The indigenous North American culture
would certainly have been driven extinct

had it not been for a survivalist
movement, founded upon
the urgency of the dilemma
and the resiliency of an ancestral religion.

Crazy Horse,
the great Oglala shaman, saw
what was happening to the native
soul of America. He knew
that if the spirituality of the Sioux
was to survive, the spirituality
of all First Nation peoples would have to be rescued
from the ethnological dilution
resulting from encroachment by non-native culture.

A distillation of ritual practice
down to those elements most applicable
within the slurry of an alien ethos
would manifest in the ritual of
the *Vision Quest* and
Yuwipi ceremonies.
These were among his people's last
remaining hopes of
an indigenous Americana.
These, today, continue in practice
and mystically rally at
the juncture between the past
and tomorrow.

In the holds of foreign registered ships,
European settlers smuggled
to these shores a cargo of African servitude.
With chains and with darkness,
the ship's crew watched
as they brandished their lachrymosity
that the sailors saw
as feeble justification
and slouching arrogance.
But these African importees

would also become Americans,
whether they wanted to or not,
and in their turn create
survivalists' distillation; authentic rite.
The celebration of *Kwanza*, as example,
was established with the hope of
popularizing the practices of African
ritual, ethos, and spirituality.

And so it seems a maxim that
whether we're native to this land
or come to it willingly or under duress
the condition of our presence here
is that we strive unrelentingly
to regain the essence
of what will soon become
our alien past:
Americana.

Princess Diana Meets Billy Strayhorn

My wife watches an Obama interview
while I groove in the tub
to Strayhorn's Upper Manhattan Medical Center
smack in the middle of a Covid spike
horn-blowers on unemployment
EMTs on overtime
thousands dying daily.

Like a tribe of Amazonian Pigmies
slated for extinction
I gently slap the surface
splashing on 2
then 4
then 2 . . .

Privilege gives me a towel,
I dry
and stop
lost in time's tapestry
of a sorrowfully woven future
empty of ideas
empty of hope

Suddenly, she (my wife)
begins reflecting upon a polo match
she once had to photograph;
Sara Ferguson and her attending Royals,
sexist, arrogant... drunk pigs all
who, she remembers, exemplified
American frat boy bumptiousness.

Suddenly Diana and Billy Strayhorn
become one
in the same family
of guilt and weakness
nastily akin

to the dichotomy
of heaven versus hell.

COVID Contrails

Runner huffing past
blissfully spewing aerosols
free from conscience
free from guilt
full of self and self alone

I see you coming
and scramble to don my face mask
fearing your wake,
fearing death
empty of faith that you care

A viral contrail
droplets lingering in still air
lilting in wait
lilting plague
the COVID dance macabre

Six Feet Asunder

The psychosis of loneliness
in crammed spaces crowded
or unbounded solitude
surrounded by deep dark waters
distanced by not knowing what the waters hold

      Begetting fear and paranoia

Back off
Don't breath my way
Don't speak to my face
In my face
On me

Begetting panic

I'm losing my sense of smell
I dare not breath
My brow drips
My chest binds

Six feet between
Moving in constant structures
Never colliding
No bumper-car shopping carts
No narrow aisles

Begetting singularity

We dance around each other
leading with our skulls
Left, right, sometimes unyielding
we pass and wave less
and less as this thing wears on

Musicians streaming from home

now playing every night
Some ganging-up
forming ensembles
via teleconferencing

Others hollering out windows

World-wide this din
everywhere

What if plants could self-quarantine?

Imagine:
Withering vines not climbing
Leaves wilting in place not falling
Roots unbunching and drying

Germs protecting themselves from other germs
All of nature repelling
Like similar charges
Six feet asunder

In The Face of Darkness

Languishing in New Orleans' summer sauna
under a "stay at home" order isolated
from social pulse and flow; direction.
No clear path forward in a maze of crumpled maps.
No ladder, no secret hatch.
But it's always been that way here,
with its reverence for entropy
and bliss making alike.
Like the famous Twin Towers faller,
striking a relaxed pose as he plummeted deathward,
We parade in the face of darkness.

Beside the Mask

Under the mask
his breath, to him,
smelled like death.
It worried and depressed him.
It wasn't going away,
even possibly getting worse.
He sank in a cross-legged puddle
of self-pity and hopelessness.

It was either he quit drinking
or quit playing.
He placed his trombone
back in its case.
Or would it read something like:
"Nonchalantly, he placed
his trombone back ... "?

     The dilemma of vocabulary
     is overusing it thus preventing
     the reader from painting
     the scene in their own hues;
     minimal is more engaging
     than emotive by inviting
     the reader to apply
     their own personal sense
     and emotion to the picture
     presented them.

The trombone lay silent
Encased, beside his mask.

I'd Lived in the City Shuttered

I'd lived in the city shuttered before,
after the Federal flood knocked the holy hell
out of an already knocked down people.
The French Quarter draped in plywood.
Canal street an echoless canyon.
The Mississippi River glassed over.
The only sound: A lone tomcat
howling as he hunts for rats
in the sewers down Decatur St.

This time's not much different
except one knows
that this time it's the same
everywhere.

Pantsdrunk in Paradise

Pantsdrunk in Paradise
the children finally gone
to places of their own accord
finally we're alone
to argue about which channel
or what to eat

another cork, and another

then another hand
and we switch
to cable news
wallow inebriated
inane discourse
nodding off unresolved

Growing Broken as One

Man woos his prospect,
a surrendering impostor
supplicating, orderly,
that she may slyly,
cleverly take
control

The plumage
The bangles
The promise kept
The promise owing
    acknowledgedly accrued

And as providence stretches,
they each fade within the other,
blurring honor with venality,
languor with lust.

Then, before age burns amok
—fate with no remedy,
they languish apiece,
growing broken
as one

C pedal

The   v e r t e x   between
two   opposing   vortices:
fear   a n d   anticipation,
spinning   in   opposite   directions
opposed,   e x p a n d i n g   outward
from   a   single   point,
a confluence   where   everything   flips.

B-7   *D major triad*

Approaching   that moment,
one worried,   one hopeful,
anguishing,   blissful,
over having no control   or thrilling at the adventure.

Bb7   *E major triad*

Driven by resentment,   ungrudgingly grateful;
saturnine,   blithesome.
the grudgesome goodbye,   embracing an unjudging welcome.

A-7b5   *F# major triad*

Desperate in her loss   while awed and assured he finds himself,

she gathers her legacy
she leaps,

Ab7

Furiously fleeing
her past turns ashen,
the shorts in her system prevail

G-7

A policy of exhaustion,
death's held-over banquet,

Gb7

Malcontentment worms its way in
the muse shuns the bone

F major7

he jettisons his last regret,
he falls.

G# major triad

he dives, deeply inspired,
his memories made,
his charge electrified.

A# major triad

invigorated verve,
life's impromptu picnic.

C major triad

as joy paints pink,
as a rose scrim glows.

D major triad

Vertex Glass *(Modified Haibun)*

      addiction to social media
people bowing to their cell phones
        everywhere in public
hence they don't see each other in the moment.

vertex glass
palmed in praying hands
two worlds drawn
as menus, maps, and "friends" rend

Gold to Gold *(Modified Haibun)*

      an epoch of attainability
when more people than not dreamt of promise
        now lost to elite corporatists
leaving no path upward for the greater static caste

hope's day reigned
in reach, spanning greed
gold to gold
lay now horizons of wood

Drifting *(Modified Haibun)*

      drifting
cars spinning donuts
        in byways and intersections
hillbilly hot-rod behavior reappropriated in the 7th ward

rubber screams
sirens to folk's ears
carving "O"s
with hands on fenders witness

Busted *(Modified Haibun)*

        knocking,
an unannounced visitor
        at the door
sends the inhabitants scrambling to escape

knuckles rap
hail without warning
threshold met
routing secreters afar.

Wasted Offering *(Modified Haibun)*

a fish
placed as a greeter's gift
decays on the doorstep
of a cottage wherein a vegan has recently moved

old man's trout
swaddled at the door
left rotting
aside a fleshless kitchen

ABOUT THE AUTHOR

Mark McGrain is an artist working in the media of new music, jazz, improvisation, composition, and performance. He is also a poet, educator, and author. Dividing his time between New Orleans and Mexico City, he continues to perform, write, and teach as a creator without borders.   A former faculty member at the prestigious Berklee College of Music in Boston, he authored the text Music Notation (Hal Leonard pub.). His musical compositions and performances have been featured on NPR, PBS, and have enjoyed critical acclaim in the U.S. and international jazz radio markets. Subscribing to a philosophy of continued action enables life continued, he and his photojournalist wife, Cheryl Gerber, enjoy the longevity offered by five shared children, six grandchildren and a cat named Joan Didion.

Omnia mutantur, nihil interit.
(Everything changes, nothing perishes.)

--Ovid (43 BC - 17 AD)
from Metamorphoses, book XV